"*How to Hold a Pebble* is a work of remarkable intellect. With empathy and playfulness, with startle and delight, Jaspreet Singh explores the fragility, beauty, and sorrow of the dreaming and waking worlds. These poems will continue to toll inside you. At times, they will turn you inside out."
—DONNA KANE, author of *Orrery*, 2020 Governor General's Literary Award finalist

"As Rilke's archaic torso was to Modernism, so is Jaspreet Singh's pebble to our late-Anthropocene literary moment. Instead of beholding the high, White ideal of 'pure' stone, we must hold the earthy, water-worn pebble. It may or may not be too late to change our lives; still, we must take the pebble in hand, steward what remains of the multifarious planet Singh both mourns and celebrates. The poems keen and dance—and amazingly, offer comfort. Humor resides here, in the polyphonic play within and among languages, as well as vital guidance: 'It [is]/impossible/to go back/the same way/we … entered'; 'Keep creating disorder, live, do not simply versify the rhetoric of empire.'"
—NATANIA ROSENFELD, author of *Wild Domestic* and *The Blue Bed*

"Jaspreet Singh distills, reveals and honors our complex relationship with the planet, from habitation to occupation, from the exquisite to the aching. His poems are mercurial and revelatory, and are always things of deep beauty."
—ANNE KENNEDY, author of *The Sea Walks into a Wall* and *The Darling North*

"For those paying attention, Singh demonstrates the monumental task of mindfulness. He enacts the quiet appreciation of a pebble while facing up to the tragedies we have made of the world. Through lenses of science, art, and history, he stares down colonialism's aftermath, environmental breakdown, and the collapse of intimacy. Despite often wishing to forget, this thoughtful poet holds to the necessity of being 'a believer / in the task of witnessing.' Like him, we must resist the urge to blink."
—JOHN BARTON, author of *We Are Not Avatars* and *Lost Family*

BOOKS BY JASPREET SINGH

NOVELS

Face (2022)
Helium (2013)
Chef (2008)

MEMOIR

My Mother, My Translator (2021)

POETRY

How to Hold a Pebble (2022)
November (2017)

SHORT STORIES

Seventeen Tomatoes: Tales from Kashmir (2004)

How to Hold a Pebble

POEMS

Jaspreet Singh

NeWest Press

Library and Archives Canada Cataloguing in Publication
Title: How to hold a pebble / Jaspreet Singh.
Names: Singh, Jaspreet, 1969– author.
Description: Series statement: Crow said poetry | Poems.
Identifiers: Canadiana (print) 20210379499 | Canadiana (ebook) 20210379510 | ISBN 9781774390535 (softcover) | ISBN 9781774390542 (EPUB)
Classification: LCC PS8637.I53 H69 2022 | DDC C811/.6—DC23

Board editor: Jenna Butler
Editor: Laurie D. Graham
Book design: Natalie Olsen, Kisscut Design

NeWest Press acknowledges the Canada Council for the Arts, the Alberta Foundation for the Arts, and the Edmonton Arts Council for support of our publishing program. This project is funded in part by the Government of Canada. ❧ NeWest Press acknowledges that the land on which we operate is Treaty 6 territory and a traditional meeting ground and home for many Indigenous Peoples, including Cree, Saulteaux, Niitsitapi (Blackfoot), Métis, and Nakota Sioux.

NeWest Press

201, 8540 – 109 Street   Edmonton, Alberta   T6G 1E6
780.432.9427
www.newestpress.com

No bison were harmed in the making of this book.
Printed and bound in Canada   1 2 3 4 5   24 23 22

For Helmut Weissert, earth scientist

— Pebbles cannot be tamed
to the end they will look at us
with a calm and very clear eye

Zbigniew Herbert

CONTENTS

HOW

TO

HOLD

A

SIX MONTHS AGO

Walking by Mount Yamnuska
nothing remained of my sense
of smell. Pine resin no longer
in the air. Was it invention
of another anxiety? Some brand
new todesfuge?

On the tip of my tongue stands
the Anthropocene
I inhaled a deep green
needle my hand plucked
from a lodgepole pine

Nothing. I broke
the needle, held it to
my nostrils. I could
smell again
and looked
up. The raven

acknowledged the return with two
little love pantoums
meant to linger
within me

They linger

I MUST LEARN AGAIN

I must learn again to be
tactile, the way I was
with the semal tree
in the yard   The tree
was a bristle
of colours   an invitation
I touched   and was touched
in return   The tree absorbed
that child the way it absorbs
a portion of visible   light
I must learn
again how to hold   a pebble
make contact with the simplest
things   I want
to unknow that a pebble
carries the whole
history of earth
I want to feel it again
as a simple thing
That one   That pebble
now in my hand

SECOND SNOW IN EDMONTON

Looking outside
I am half-
thinking about an old news-
paper report: on Kafka's
birthday (in 1982
or '84) a man woke up
in his pyjamas, tethered
himself to a lawn chair
tied to 42 helium balloons
and simply flew away

On TV they keep showing aerial
bombing of a distant city
on the edge
of a desert

SILEN E

Brecht said What times are these
in which a conversation about trees
is almost a crime

Brech sai Wha time ar thes
n whic conversatio abou tree
i almos crim

Brec sa Wh tim a the
whi conversati abo tre
almo cri

Bre s W ti th
wh conversat ab tr
alm cr

Br t t
w conversa a t
al c

B
convers
a

conver

conve

conv

con

co

c

A K A - B O

Another language has joined *foraminifera*
Fossils   In the calcitic ruins

echoes
          cannot say
enough

A wayward poem inherits
epochal unconsciousness

Of loss   no scale   remains   no seawall

A child uses a phrasal verb

Come back

ALBEDO I

Last night a saxifrage broke the teeth of darkness

The dog jumped like a dump truck

The cat skinned a Poe

The fish ate some second-hand plastic

Mount Assiniboine ice cores puddled in a climate lab

Fukushima slept in a fungal unconformity

Olivines rained on an elephant-headed Ganesha

In Korea a piano nearly revived moribund tomatoes

The last known of a frog species died

And I blamed an albedo in a bad dream

Today there are no trains in Bremen; an email from the institute alerted me. A team is diffusing a World War II bomb near the city centre. The bomb was found by construction workers doing routine digging.

Yesterday there was train traffic. Yesterday I shadowed a glaciologist, who gave me a tour of the ice-core archive. I was allowed to touch an ice core, its traces of a volcanic eruption several thousand years ago. A few days earlier, during a similar shadowing, a deep-sea post-doc allowed me to touch a sediment core, its traces of the end-Cretaceous mass extinction sixty-six million years ago.

Before I walked back to the train station, the post-doc also showed me a large collection of marine organisms less than one millimetre in size. "Foraminifera," she said. "They have such a small life span."

Of all the fossils I have encountered—vertebrate and invertebrate— these tiny calcium carbonate shells stir me the most. Porous and dead, beautiful witnesses.

The bomb was successfully diffused, said the sprightly TV host in German. On ICE Bahn—the intercity express—the coffee tasted better.

DARWISH
— a ghazal —

The only decent way to restore loss is to brew coffee like Darwish
Uncanny aromas will humanize you if you brew it like Darwish

The climate is changing, not even an ear bone left of old species
Stop bothering typhoons. Simply make coffee new like Darwish

Shall I stir counter-clockwise, up, down, slowly undo clockwise?
Don't let it sink! Master the technique. Screw coffee like Darwish

You mean, when flames forage a zoo, curfew nothing?
What is the hurry? Smell slurp taste slow coffee like Darwish

Eggs sizzle in the fry pan. Why, habibi, why are so few for Others' truth?
Remove all traces of untraces and see through the coffee, like Darwish

And I, Preet, wonder why the world turns blue sipping this hospitable liquid?
Double-handedly undress the limpid mug. Drink coffee like Darwish

INSPIRATION

His friends took
him to a mountain
in Yoho National
Park thinking
he would
mutter the first
lines of a pro-
found poem, and all
he said was *This
seems like an ideal place
to eat gobhi-aloo*

WHYTE AVENUE

A woman is looking at a mural
in Edmonton, freshly painted
It is not a bustling street
But some of the others
passing by (that couple
fresh out of a red
Toyota) join her
in the looking

Now there are six
of us—two men
three women and a child
I cannot tear myself
from the lacerated
pavement. I feel
I have entered the mimetic
desire of the first woman
looking at the mural
painted freshly in Edmonton
or I am simply

      outside
      the frame

This is where we
might have parted
me and the woman
But times have
changed. Mural making
and watching have changed
Every day I feel
as if it is my last
on a troubled planet. I
cannot simply go
home fry eggs keep thinking
about the one fine
woman who was looking

        The whale
in the mural
is done in oil

It is a beauty
It is flying

Alive like some Melville

Makes my thoughts

move to a ship-

breaking yard

in Bangladesh

The flying whale

takes me

near a boy

scavenging

a toxic ship

      The sea is rising

  and Whyte Avenue   will make it
rise
more   will keep making
heat
to drown the whole of Chittagong

      ship graveyard

It is going to be a long night

For me

For the whale

For the boy

Who can't stop flying

ALBEDO II

A glacier at the base
of Mt. Everest lost albedo
and released its cargo: sweat-
shirts, embroidered
blackbirds, a Bolly-
wood T. Rex intact
still. Bodies with hobnailed boots

One attached to her ruck-
sack, eyes
refusing to shut, her hair
a dignified sinusoidal
wave in the wind

The twisted prairie
grass outside
my window is also play-
ing with the wind. The wind
will remain and will
soon carry us all

I half close
my eyes. Sometimes
the best way through
is to do nothing
and wait for the thaw

LITTLE BLUES

— Fraser Valley, Canada —

At times the blueberry
fields of Abbotsford
resemble little Nihangs
bobbing
in an old naa'la
in Punjab   Lord, I
love these berries
Just the right diameter
Why did you make me
taste them
only at twenty
and one? They made me
neglect cherries
peaches, fleshy dus'shehri
mangos, especially
these phul'ian phal'ian
nilli'ian bey'rian. Why
cannot I
abite them
without linking the delight-
ful event in my mouth
to hands, bodies   To the sufferings
of those who perform
the work   of plucking
in this twenty-
first century? If only
you existed, Lord,
you would have
found a fair way
to sweeten
your little things

ART OF SPRING

To be alone in spring
is a high crime
as snow melts away
from my balcony

Alone in the apart-
ment and still able
to warm a poem
out of this loneliness

It's still a crime
Like some lance-tipped machine
at a dry mountain resort
giving birth

to artificial snow

À TOUTE ÉPREUVE

When I woke up
a fly woke up
from the same pillow
Accompanied my flip-
flops to the kitchen
I drank a glass
of hydrogen
dioxide   The fly
startled by sudden
electric bulb igniting
Broke the silence
flying   non-
pragmatically
over a Miró-
Éluard art book long
gone out of print
Open at a headless
page next to two onions
and sharp teeth
of garlic   I felt a prickle
My eardrums clicked
as if someone were
sequencing a DNA
sample   The fly was still
gluey   carrying
a mild grudge   I saw it land
on Miró's ambiguous
colour shapes and Éluard's
Je n'ai jamais changé
Collaborating with
two great dadas

of the 20th century
Twice in strong
argumentation with them
about geo-ethics and God
knows what   All
through the night
I observed she? he? them? it?
Unable to go back
to the cold sheets of my bed

THE DREAM

—for Julio Cortázar—

A knock on my door
at midnight. They found the
bodies of my poems on the desk. They
did not take them away

How indifferent, I thought
It was then one of them
returned to confiscate
the fear I had seen in a handful of compost

The moment they left
the desert walked in, took over
my house one room at a time
It occurred to me I would not be

needing the keys anymore

ATTACHMENT STYLE

To you I am attached
not like compartments
in a train
More the way a postcard
from the Silk Road
is attached to a wall
with Scotch tape

A child can separate us,
an anxious guest, a gust
from the window, or
the simple everyday
of a bed being made
by someone who knows
us far too little

I makc no complaints. Like you
I will continue to enjoy
our precarious union
in this brightening room
until a moth flutters
wings in Amritsar
and lost mulberries
are found. Until
a yipping

tiger or a new suffering
a mild
  tremor in Bali
knocks down light
  bulbs, and

a drop of brandy
  dissolves the lip balm
and an odd
  airless scent
shakes my
  threads and the last silk-
worm utters

. . . .

[rip here]

INFIDELITY

I left a signed copy
of *Eros the Bittersweet*
by Anne Carson
under my beloved's pillow
She fell

in love with AC

      All through the night she
translated the poet
into a radical
storm, a polar
vortex loning
          inside a polar
          vortex. She figured—

      the two halves of an apple
                        by not
      merging into

      one

      create lasting
      percussion

Sanskrit to me, I said, and she kissed me
never again
the usual way. Did I

deserve this bad

      weather?

She wanted me
to unimagine
what spring does to cherry trees

You have become an air
conditioner—she said—cooling
the room
by heating

the planet evermore

BIRTHDAY

Snow diagrams
on freezing rain
Unsteady lozenges

The little ono-
matopoeic teapot
shook in her hand

I heard
Even Sylvia Plath
stopped at thirty
She spoke of
certainties like that

Twenty mountains
we counted
in the Sierra Nevada
White blankets   Solemn
mandalas   invisible now

The double glass
reflected half a
blood-red candle
about to be snuffed
to prolong its life

Sorry   I said
No   I am sorry   she said
and the null moment
passed

KATHASARITSAGAR

The DNA test informed me that stories
run in my family

My great-great-grandmother was a doll
with a horse lover

And my great-great-grandfather murdered
a serpent in order to save himself from
transforming into an acacia tree

They sold their children to a travelling circus
which channelled the family
into invention of wings, fire, and five
minutes a day near weightlessness

The children promised themselves as they fell
in love, we will not again
make the same mistake
not have the same run-in with stories

THINGS, LISTEN

Things, listen to me
as only you are
able to
Perhaps
the *S*
in my family
name was simply
a typo of child-
hood and I
really am a thing
among things

A pebble a bone a letter
opener a dancing
girl~~~~perhaps
a rusted pin found
in a vanishcd

undeciphered 4000-

year-old city   of semi-arid sand

              and

monsoonlessness

EVERYTHING IS IN ORDER

—a ghazal, 2019—

Whatever you do, defy the sweet rhetoric of empire
Bleed that big melon, liquefy the rhetoric of empire

Only the unexpected, the unknown will justify the future
Reinvent language, read Césaire, demystify the rhetoric of empire

Investigate traces, dwellings, oral histories, testify in moving voice
Hesitation will only let the dead be used to buy the rhetoric of empire

Amritsar Massacre marks a painful hundred today, and you fifty
Learn from Bhagat Singh, disqualify newspeak, the rhetoric of empire

Colonizing barbarians will quantify you yet again, co-opt, vilify your people
Cops in the head, emollients may super-magnify the rhetoric of empire

Jaspreet, framed photos of Frantz Fanon will only beautify in time
Keep creating disorder, live, do not simply versify the rhetoric of empire

DIAGRAM OF A BLINK

The twentieth century disappeared
Leaving its crimes behind
In the twenty-first

For nascent heartbeats
Of CRISPR, revived wooly mammoths
And unwoundable androids
To figure

Good
Afternoon, Anthropocene!
I say while
The book in my hand
Takes a nap and my bathtub
Goes bone dry

FEBRUARY

The world is a happy place,
said the yellow-cab cabbie. Some look
for sadness and find sadness

The streets and avenues
of Edmonton were white and
minus forty-nine

Like traffic lights we switched
to Punjabi. But he was less
funny in mothertongue, even
less wise. I did not mind. I was in
Edmonton. The streets and avenues
white and minus forty-nine and I was

soon going to boil
an egg or buy a pound
of greenhouse baby

strawberries
packed in a bag of
unhappy plastic

MELANCHOLIA

my Melancholia is a fat Buddha smiling incapable

my Melancholia is a stale pale ale pillow

my Melancholia is a house on stilts that was

my Melancholia is the unoriginality of melancholia

my Melancholia is a crooked cello on a solitary chair

my Melancholia is an Ordovician pebble with a Lorca face

my Melancholia is dog days wagging

my Melancholia is a diminutive for ship breaking

my Melancholia is a feral kinship with darkness

my Melancholia is erasure of puns from Punjabi

my Melancholia is an osteoporotic coral

my Melancholia is a fatal thought attack

my Melancholia is unmulchable shame

my Melancholia is Saturn's toe ring

my Melancholia is mistranslation of rarely inherited sound

MAMA

Mama, what happens to holy books
With time

They grow old

Mama, what happens to forests

They become phrases
In Prakrit or Sanskrit

You have to change your life

SOME PHOTONS

On a magazine cover—Victoria Ocampo's eyes

Black-and-white twentieth-century Rio de Janeiro
Ojos in Spanish
Augen in German
Akhaan in Punjabi, my mother's eyes
exactly like eyes in the photo. Exactly like
your eyes this Victoria Ocampo's eyes, says the woman
reading the magazine at the clinic

and some ghostly photons passed right through

MAKING WAVES

—Amritsar, Punjab, Holocene—

Sweaty zebra crossings

I recall the woman with a
steel bracelet buying a
holy book from the sidewalk
vendor

The man in cyan blue
was double saying
to his springy grandchild
*This is where you come
if you ever get lost*

No recall

of whose lap
I was on when
I touched my first
Golden Temple

What was *that*

bright outdoor

room like? As good
as vowels in prayer? Was it around
then (pushed by a relative
        or tradition)

I took my first long-exposure
steps in the dukh
bhan'jani amrit sarovar? Ma was
telling me about Baba Deep Singh

when I saw a doll
making waves
in the rectangled waters, bobbing
sadly, showing
its mutilations. The thing

is I do not recall
the original plastic
eyes, ears, and nose
but its hair was golden

Years later a grieved
well-preserved voice explained
One needs strong night-
vision devices

to detect the chunnis

the awakening turbans, toys

and scuffed shoes of the dead

H.G. GLYDE'S MURAL

—University of Alberta—

Before the talk on *Poetry after Auschwitz*
we looked around for the head
of Czesław Miłosz (1911–2004)
donated by the Polish Cultural Society
to the library that stands
on four long forgotten libraries

Miłosz's bushy eyebrows provided
a moment of lucidity
by the building entrance. But
we strayed, stood below—
Alberta History made by a "full
man" Henry George Glyde (1906–1998)

What was he thinking?

Glyde, British-born, somewhat
renowned, painted the Indigenous
as if they had only half a face
half a head, no names, no land

The entire reading room smelled
of fermenting fruit in compost bins

My friend removed
her loafers and gloves, meditated
on Indigeneity, on de-

colonizing the academy
on contemporary activism

on *pessimism of the intellect*
and optimism of the will
blended slowly
with the gliding head
of Czesław Miłosz:
you see how I try / to reach with words /
  what matters the most / and how I fail?

    a murmur, then

only silence spoke, and although there was no alarm
no smoke, no flame, we looked
for the nearest fire exit. It was

impossible

to go back

the same way

we had entered

He took us to the grey zone
where he takes everyone
whose name is
Mary or Mohammed
and presses them between
glass slides like everyday
insects

During free time he hides
his face, reads Pliny
the Elder, Brothers Grimm, Siddhartha
Mukherjee. Blogs
on eugenics. Russian
novels, always third-person

His gross monthly salary
a scandal although
health insurance
covers plastic
surgery, a decent
dental, travel
allowance, a tan
in Cuba
or some other
grey zone

UNCONTAINABLE

1

At the end of the tunnel
     not light
but a red dwarf

1.1

On CBC *Late Night*
a man
was talking to a bird   The last
speaker of an ancient language   The man was me

1.11

I am naked
The cat is as curious
        as AI
I must apprehend how to return
the pebble's gaze
It wants me   to become its ring

1.111

Unsure if I love
Musca domestica sitting far
from us   The wind discovers pain
is a consequence of making
contact   The elm
caved in   The dolphins
in Venice
turned out   fakes

2

The lie of a new migrant
Is different from the lie
Of an old migrant   Hence
The misunderstandings

3

Here compost tragedies
Here recycle comedies
Here ferment memories
Like blood oranges

3.3

We feed chickens
with tandoori chicken
bone shit tantalum   We are
all the hyper-
objects extracted and dumped   We perform
the event as if it were a thing a well-oiled machine
could fix

4

Time has come   to turn the object
of every sentence into its subject   Revisit old allegories
                    Making sounds
            a pebble makes   when it drops us

5

We didn't open Pandora's

dumpster   It was always

exposed   The walls

of the uncontainable were made

Out of language

in which the "third world" was told

You will catch up

Now the "first world"

fears it as dead

certainty   It will

catch up with the third

BY THE BANKS OF A VANISHING RIVER
—Palmerston North, New Zealand—

Manawatu in old Maori—a heart stilled along the way

Shimmering waters *most polluted in western hemisphere*

Cedars, ratas, miros stand despite the river survey

To colonials the town but a righteous railway crossing

Foxton Harbour line blackholes timber mills in its fold

Manawatu in old Maori—a heart stilled along the way

Gone the station. Only the grandfather clock remains

Rugby. Jesus. Resurrected Huia bird. Municipal art

Cedars, ratas, miros stand despite the river survey

Air Force bagpipes sacralize the ones gone far away

Earthquake in Christchurch. Walls nothing but shards

Manawatu in old Maori—heart stilled along the way

Teenagers race Gatsby cars. Burger King grills every day

Hope lies with modern-day wakas, windturbines charging Quixotes

Manawatu in old Maori—heart spilled along the way

Cedars, ratas, miros still stand despite the river survey

THE ZOO

My parents visited
Calgary. When dust
settled I hailed
a cab to see otters

A soft-spoken
Punjabi, our taxi-
wallah disapproved of
my idea of fun. Zoos
a waste
of money and good
weather, he said—

Back home Mummy-
and-Papa encounter
unlocked life
on every other road
avenue and gali

Have you forgotten
an elephant, he said
a camel
a monkey
a black bear, a coiled poisonous
snake, a bearded goat, a water
buffalo? Have you no

Memory of eggs
of sauropodinosaurs
found by labourers
by the watch factory?

No yaad'an of soft
worms on mulberry
trees making
silk? Kir'e makor'e
those fun-tastic bats?

Vultures? Sudden soul/
rooh pleasing peacocks?

North America and
Europe used to display
non-white
people in zoos
Hope you heard

of this show
of dehumanization?

What's the difference?
Another 24/7
horror. Do they want to be there
the ones we call
animals?

Take my advice, he said
Show respected parents the Athabasca
Glacier before it melts

ਦਲੀਪ ਸਿੰਘ

—Duleep Singh, 1838–1893—

one wrong sound and you're shelved in the Native Literature section
resistance writing
a mad Indian

—MARILYN DUMONT

Unconformity is a gap   It appears
when large chunks   of time
disappear from the geological record

Record it:
I live in a place
named after the youngest
daughter of Queen Victoria

In Alberta
mountains quadripple a person's
idea of a mountain
Clear lakes play pebbly chess
with moraines and katabatic wind

Does it matter if half the globe
remains unaware
of this land's deep
condensed fossil witnesses, or
oil held by its sands, or
the approximate location

of sites where collective memory skips time

Or the meaning of the Punjabi name *Dalip*
(mispronounced *Duleep*)

Or stunning properties of graphite diamond
Buckminsterfullerene, all allotropes
of carbon, or traces
of history, which is neither
a mountain nor light

Write it down: Koh-i-noor was
stolen—
Queen Victoria stole
the diamond
from a ten-year-old
boy in Punjab. She forgot
to record the loot
and recut the 'gift'
as a crown jewel. Princess

Alberta was around a year old then

Like a fairy-tale figure
Alberta's mother also stole
the ten-year-old boy from his beloved
mother, Rani Jindan of Punjab
Took him past seven
seas to a fog of an island
(The archive tells us that his house
was on occupied
land   body, language stolen
music, lutes, rababs
also.) As if enough
was not enough
his mother too, stolen

Research question: How did they face each other
the little girl and the little boy, when they grew up?

As for me, yes, there is a bit
of emotion. Sometimes nothing
at all. Do not
interpret this as unconformity
or a thing unable
to fit the pH
of metaphor. I am
in a noisy bar
with a fountain
pen, a Moleskine, four
empty glasses. We are
surrounded by fogs
of light

On the TV the new Duchess
of Sussex—

I thought about it
        because
they made me
        think about it

I thought about it

I thought
as much as the fog
allowed me to think

DOUBLE BOND

Science transforms me into one single
person. Art makes me
many. But really I do not buy
the two-culture trap
I am a unit of sound
two charmed particles of light
I am early

        music

      a wild wonder

       in the ears

        of mitochondrial DNA

I am a   half
finished   utopia

YOU A GENIUS

Tomorrow I will be   the face
Of the morning
For two full hours   I will
Breathe toxic
Air of Switzerland

But   Switzerland is so small
It does not contribute much

So why not cut the whole
World into little Switzerlands

MIRABEL

Although the names of vegetables and some fruits changed
(from one variety of English to another) the trouble
with moving to Canada was simply
not what my mother/father imagined
I thought it would be a 'saf'far'
a journey different from going
to Saturn. From rings
of benzene to toluene
in a slightly different chemistry
department in a slightly different
city where snow fell just like
the pouncing leopards
of my Himalayan childhood
Set in parentheses the arrival
at Mirabel Airport
Focus on the young man lost
on *de Bullion* street
See 'gavaatcha':
Punjabi for a young male hopelessly
lost. Or 'gavaatchi chirri'—*lost like a sparrow*
orbiting round and round before
he perches between chenar and maple
by some unremarkable accident

DEEP TIME NUT

The scientists said their little telescopes were going
to photograph a black hole
Other than briefly
looking up all I could
muster was Roland
Barthes—his terrestrial
    studium

and *punctum*. The physicists
said at best
the halo of a hole
could be grabbed
by edgy devices
pulsating together
like a fishing net

What does the fish
look like? I asked

Get ready, they said
It will curve
   and curve
you towards its unflick-
ering shadow and you
will grow young
trying to locate
lost memories-socks-
spoons-pets in some non-
    beautiful side
of a deep vanished lub-dub   PEA   NUT

OZYMANDIAS II

In Slovenia, a bone flute

and recently in a cave in Spain
a human undarked
more Neanderthal
art: the diagram
for a game
of noughts and crosses

Enigmatic symbols on raw
carbonate with red
pigment. *Aesthetic sensibility—older*
than 63,000 years?

After the find
all one can say
about *Sapiens—*
More con
artists than artists

For a while now we spread
myths about the Neanderthals. Lack
            of art made them
disappear from the face and ass of Earth

Disappeared despite art
conjecture expunged
as ambiguous, as mimicry, at best
as irony

Noughts and crosses aside
while one awaits
deeper scientific scrutiny
of hand-stencils, *craziness*
DNA, it is hard
not to see through the mesh

that is the future

Most astonishing
despite constant pull and push (and
because of it) one may
continue incubating objects—glowing
layers of beauty out of bones

until the very end, and
that also is the future

MOUNTAINS

At some point I stopped saying 'When I arrived in North
America.' As inadequate as 'When I left South
Asia.' These markers of space-
time felt like someone
else's narrative. Even when I switched
to the longish
'When I moved from place
where genocides took place
to place where genocides took
place,' it felt not close
enough, as if pain-
ful history was being
aestheticized. Better say I moved
from mountain X to mountain Y
and I can live
with that

ਪਤਾ

—after Cavafy—

ਤੂੰ ਕਿਹਾ ਸੀ, "ਮੈਂ ਪੈਰੀਪੈਟੈਟਕਿਪਨ ਛੱਡਣ ਜਾ ਰਿਹਾ ਹਾਂ । ਇੱਕ ਮੁਲਕ, ਇੱਕ ਸ਼ਹਿਰ, ਇੱਕ
ਗੁਆਂਢ, ਇੱਕ ਸੜਕ, ਇੱਕ ਰੁੱਖ, ਇੱਕ ਘਰ . . .

You said, "I am going to give up being peripatetic. Choose a country,
a city, a neighbourhood, a street, a tree, a house. So scattered I feel.
I have moved some 51 times, 51 addresses in all. My things are scattered.
Boxes everywhere. Even my nostalgia is multiple. Fragmented. Retro-
retrospective. My bitterness, multiple bitternesses. I am aging and
things keep accumulating. I cannot discard the stuff—for I have also
become the custodian of objects the dead in my life keep leaving
behind. I have simply wasted, ruined my life."

"Don't forget, your joy, accretion of multiple joys," I said, as we parted.
"Hope it all works out . . . ਘਬਰਾਇਆ ਨਾ ਕਰ!"

"Nothing will. Nothing will ever work out. Everything will remain just
the same. Soon it will be the 52nd, and thereafter the 104th. This moving
around gives me convulsive happiness. My only sea of happiness.
Why am I constantly trying to run away from it? To keep wander-
ing is the best choice I ever made. I will make it again. The reason
I move is to stay. The same. For once, I know what I am going to
do at the new place. Perfuse. Make lasting beauty before imminent
heatwaves. Melt."

ENDINGS

—for Ana Blandiana—

She photographed
eighteen bridges, nine
bakeries, that strange
mural by the Mexican
bar. She photographed rain
and the city
in rain. It was the finest
rain of our lives
because we were in love
and we did not know
it was soon going
to end. Her city was
filled with force
and beauty of rain
Drawn to ruins and
abandoned power
stations, she photographed
their crumbling splendour
in rain, and although
we did not know
where we would go
after the eviction
we were happy
She photographed empty
apartments in rain, elms swaying
in the wind, night
shimmering in the streets
intersections in rain, and we
were ungrammatically happy
much in love
and we so enjoyed the rain

BOREAL REALISM

The diagram of the Future
is two diagrams
sutured
as one—Bee-ness
of Bitumen
Bitumen-ness
of Bees

This is my first
non-cliché, me the person
trapped in hexagons
of clichés. The one who keeps
saying Life
is a gift Life is a gift

BEAUTY
—for A.M. and H.B—

We were waiting for the tube as they say
in London My friend
a non-binary math-e-matician
in irreversible love with the ir-
rational *e*
In blue he diagrammed
on his dry palm
the earthly origins of Euler
Number 2.718281828459045235360287471352 7 . . .
smiling, trying a wee
bit harder each time
as if idealizing the never-finishedness of l-o-v-
e. But all I could think of
was whether there was a number I
felt so passionate about. Not a single
one in the world, no rational prime
transcendental. No fraction square
root series. Not even
a random taxi licence plate
The kind Ramanujan spoke of
dying in a hospital bed in London
Zero?
At this point
he drew a warm tender dot-
ted line on the other palm
a hanging
necklace, a catenary, his fingers
shook a bit, perhaps it was
a rumble. I heard
"canary" and nearly fell in the gap
or flew out of joy because now

I was in love
not with the presence of numbers
but with the burrowed tunnels
of their absence
As relationships go I found myself
telling my friend on the red line my relationship
with numbers *was*
truly marvellous, all of them, all of them

THE DEAD RETURN

The dead return when you try
out their recipes
They watch you eat
with the same amusement
the way you watch a cat
consume phad thai
The way you observe
in silence a clay golem
And all along
you thought the high
loaf of finding them was near
yellow fallen leaves   just outside
an alfresco or a
glassed fair
trade café   How sobering
the way they admire empty
white bags
flutteringly in the bare branches
of a wintering chestnut

Do not stare at them
or talk about comets
dark matter   planetary
conjunctions
Nor comment on *the* recipe
Their secret
is they are
more than tongue-tied
facial expressions
of passing clouds   Shy
as they are
they might run

and hide away

in the white
of noodles, or in humming
molecular ribbons
of banned plastic

M U

The filmmaker Yasujiro Ozu lies buried next
to his mother in Kitakamakura, near Tokyo. On the stone
there is no name, only
mu—
'emptiness,' 'silence,' 'stillness'

Most of his films had circular
endings, and so did his
life. He was
born on December 12 in 1903 and died
on his birthday in 1963. I was nothing
then. I was born a few years later. Now I am
able to make a long snake
with a small knife
when I peel an apple

WALKING

Sometimes I walk past buildings long
deceased, the ones that can't exist
as ruins

When I take little steps
my eye doesn't feel out
of place

  I walk

and   time   repairs
my ozone   I smell
layers of rock
        an alibi
of a memory   soaks
 me up like a consoling cyclone

I go over tyreless cars
I go through fog
         and fog
chimes   I walk through people's
chatter, laughter, cycles of melanin
sweaty melancholic faces
and everyone's
eyes   voices   They like my body
best when witnessed
walking   Drawn by
runnels   I walk   Repelled
I walk as well   Sometimes others
accompany me, but that makes
a different walk
Through burnt forests, pebble rain-
sticks   and waiting

piles
of tender quivering surpluses
of garbage

I sing

                            lines
into existence

    by walking

  I walk through

borders, eggs, slug glugs   con-
tested histories
I walk in wrinklings of
glaciers   Dive
—I am walking—
into the deepest wild
oceans   ghost calcitic
populations
My feelers awaken clams
warm muds, Cambrian worms
late-Cretaceous plankton
                I used
to think I was so strange
Someone who inherited
a lot
of mess   Will pass on

    more

    mess

But now all falls

    into place

I was never some wayward
branch

Tree was
the wrong
metaphor

Perhaps some more
apt thing

exists for humans now

The stories we live
                Our fictions
now as powerful
as Earth's supreme
geological force
                Our things
change the way
we walk

and drown

I locate these traces along
buildings long deceased, the ones
that couldn't exist as ruins

WHO LIT THE FIRE?

Truth lies sandwiched between layers of rock. Between lives lived. Sparks created. Anthropo-unseens.

For some the new epoch is all crime and little punishment. For others little crime, all punishment.

"How can we erupt a feral dialogue in the dark times? i.e. Impenetrable darkness in an age of brightly lit cities seawalled with reeds and enigmatic foam."

Yes, a scene in our Anthropocenes.

One must learn again. How to hold a pebble. Learn again. What lies between pebbles.

AN OLIVINE

Olivines were found among
hot matter
spewed out by the volcano
Cumbre Vieja
in La Palma

Olivines attract jewellers
parables
also scientists, who might
use them to trap
oceanic and atmospheric CO_2

I sit by
the caldera
Heat fills
my eyes, my eyes
are heat's eyes

Two hands
digging

Two ears
listening

Olivines make use of us

to go where they want to go

They are worse
than words!

They sleep with eyes
open and walk backwards

weathering
themselves constantly

They face their mother
earth with reverence

Not keen to find out the age of my
house, only verifying the age
of the mountain behind

We stared   as mindfully they voiced:

you never look at us
from the place
from which we see you

One olivine
persuaded me to delay
dying

It has sequestered me

It is under my tongue, it is my

tongue now

NATURECULTURE

The Englishman was wrong
They only half
fuck you up
your mum and dad
and leave

the other half
for the rest
of the globe

They fuck up
the planet as well
More than you
can repair

Is it *joder* or *follar?*
asked the Spanish translator

C O N T A G I O N
—for K.N.—

I am waiting
for the sun
to embrace
unnecessary margaritas
of early spring (my smart-
phone zooms in
and out on the deadly aerosols)

I am waiting
for un-fake dolphins
as they approach
contagious cities. Waiting
for faces
unsuspicious, unbuttoned
glances, handmade masks
I have become so aware
of my own breath
its lessness

Quarantined
by corners
in this corner of the world
(Once it was known
as *the* centre)
Cobwebs cling to me
hoping I wouldn't take them
elsewhere

I can't even lift
a hand
to point
a finger

at my species
and at my selves

I commit
mighty crimes to hoard bare
necessity, toilet
rolls, an exponential
bottle of liquid
soap. I am waiting
for this never before
posthumous feeling
to end. So that I can

come back again
Nothing
changed   all
things seachanged

ENTANGLEMENTS

—The human-non-human hum in late capitalism—

Up the slopes of Sleeping Buffalo
        Canadian
Rockies   They look like hunger

artists   The dead trees starved

by the mountain pine beetle

Rust-coloured remnants
the needles   Un-
familiar calligraphy—tiny tunnel
entrances on the bark

Still and still

        staring   I was

warned to take

cover   Harsh bugle

        rutting sounds coming

from close by   a male

        fully antlered   I was almost

glued

        to my spot

The female elk's eyes
meeting mine
        I knew I was both
a danger

to them and in danger myself   She moved

her head slightly

a nimble
free will

This kind of staring
would not work
with a tiger, a lynx
or bacteria, but it was working

with wild

ungulates   On both sides

no fear   What stirrings arose

inside her?

A little bond may have
        formed
        trust esta-
blished   The calves, too, curious, even

more than the mother, felt
    safe enough to turn
    to grass   grazing

The new condition? I wondered

Later, S said, in our tunnel-like cabin
Let's talk about hope
The cabin warm and lanternish
Familiar rust-ink calligraphy
That beetle   diagram   glowed in a wall
hanging

Hope is my
vocation, I said cautiously But
as you know I practice it only
when there is no hope left

ASH IS THE PUREST EVENT

Scientists say sometimes it is easy
to mark the end
of an epoch. Catastrophes, mass
extinctions might be natural
boundaries of time
Is the Anthropocene's
mark sharp enough? Like volcanism
that ended the Permian?
The invention
of *making fire* its real beginning?

TV talk-show hosts say it is
not all doom
and gloom and try
to save the late-
night with *hope*

As if the word
were a candy
wrapper. Some sweet   (out of context)

Marcel Duchamp urinal
work of art

No, it doesn't matter, the name-
mark of the epoch. Deep down
one knows
one will always
carry it in those
cracks within
Between one's despairs
they will brighten
Hope's in-built traces

CYCLONE

—a toddler's memories, 50 years after Bhola Superstorm—

Things were falling   apart   Things
were also
                coming
together. Roots,trees,pigs,streets,bulbs,trays,milk,bed-
sheets   soilednappies

    with
            moss   that lone matador   calmly looped around
    with

heats,beaches,drums,bibs,babies   soilednappies
bed milk bulb peach street frog tree roof   root
                        coming
were also
apart Things   Things Falling   were

flew together

    its own warm   flawless   eye

swirled together

SYMBIOSIS

Plastics inside the belly of a bird

Birds inside the belly of a plastic

Plastic will continue   to fly

Into our face   faces   facings

Unstable it stands cancelled: our I-ness

The medicine the endocrinologist gave

Me is dissolving in the bottle of Evian

When everything is a symptom, how do we

Locate what is not?

CALCIUM

Perhaps I exaggerate   My loneliness

All emptiness has   entered

my bones   and left them with

o s t e o p e n i a on the verge of o s t e o p o r o s i s

Yesterday reading   about corals   "being repaired"

I felt as if   I was scanning holes

in the sea   within

FUTURE

Today I went there again
Stared at Gaia's no-longer-lavish
face. Having mastered
the grammar of small
contact-making
I said sorry to all planetary
plants and animals and
ectoplasm   my lips
unable to still   and come
to a stop
The cuttlefish wore that usual
missing link
wisdom in its eyes. The otter
and the salmon
kept unfolding the ocean's soft body
as if the only way
to keep death at bay
and pebbles holding it

tight

No way I was going
to be righteous
or sing *que sera sera*

I said sorry before
the idea of forgiveness
faded, fell out of use
flat like some meme
'I don't like you but I love you'
'I cannot wear your shirt
but I will give you my organ'

Maybe I ought to have followed
some radical path
Separated from real action
empathy is no empathy

It is easier / to imagine / an end /
to the world /
than an end / to capitalism

Would it be like drops
of water on the moon?

NO PERSON IS AN ARCHIPELAGO

—after Antonio Machado—

Show me the sea inside, especially
Minor shipwrecks. Major
Ones are no use. Right
Now if possible. To see
The sea as a woman
Is foolish. To see it
As a man (the way
This surfaces in some other
Languages) is also absurd. Let go
The desolations. Be
Easy on yourself
In the middle
Of the night. Try to
Forget to forget
To once more fall in love

GO WENT GONE

Will old age olden all the kisses
I was given
Or will they remain
Just the same
Because there are astonishments
I still want to know
The sweat of hands, for instance
Fugacity and longevity of pronouns
I want to locate
What grows
In gaps between couplings
Why erosion beautifies
Things more so
Because I am still
A body, a believer
In the task
Of witnessing. Because I feel
Compelled to remind
You at the door politely
That it is kind
Of time for
Us to kiss and say
Goodbye

NOTES

p. 7: The epigraph comes from the poem "Kamyk" by
Zbigniew Herbert, first published in *Struna swiatla* (1956).
Translated from Polish by Peter Dale Scott and Czesław Miłosz.

p. 18: Aka-Bo is an extinct language of the Andaman Islands,
a remarkable 70,000-year-old language. Boa Sr, its last speaker,
died in January 2010.

p. 49: Quote comes from Antonio Gramsci:
> *pessimism of the intellect*
> *and optimism of the will*

p. 81: According to Wentworth's (1922) grain-size classification
published in *The Journal of Geology*, sand-sized particles lie
between 62.5 microns and 2 millimetres. "Pebbles" lie between
4 millimetres and 64 millimetres.

p. 83: *You never look at me from the place from which I see you.*
See Jacques Lacan's "The Line and Light" in The Four Fundamental
Concepts of Psycho-Analysis (Norton, 1978). This page also takes its
inspiration from the work of Marina Abramović, Emmanuel Levinas,
Ludwig Wittgenstein, Donna Haraway, and Dipesh Chakrabarty's
The Climate of History in a Planetary Age (Chicago, 2021).

p. 92: Bangladesh. November 1970. Bhola Cyclone disaster.

p. 97: Fredric Jameson in his essay "Future City" (NLR, 2003):
> *Someone once said that it is easier to imagine the end of the*
> *world than to imagine the end of capitalism.*

A possible variation:
> *It is easier to imagine an end to the world than an end to human*
> *exceptionalism.*

Amitav Ghosh—in The Nutmeg's Curse (Chicago, 2021)—comes up
with the following:
> *That which is really harder to imagine than the end of the world*
> *is the end of the absolute geopolitical dominance of the West.*

ACKNOWLEDGEMENTS

First versions of some poems appeared elsewhere:

"Inspiration" in *Alberta Views*, 2019.

"Second Snow in Edmonton" in *Alberta Views*, 2018.

"You a Genius" in an *Olive Reading Series* chapbook, 2018.

"Some Photons" in *The Polyglot* 3, Edmonton, Canada, 2018.

"H.G. Glyde's Mural" in *The Polyglot* 3, Edmonton, Canada, 2018.

"Residences" in *The Polyglot* 3, Edmonton, Canada, 2018.

For known and unknown reasons I would like to thank Laurie Graham, Jenna Butler, Mark Smith, Natania Rosenfeld, Anton Kirchhofer, Anne Carson, Kim Nekarda, Lilian Robl, John Barton, Helmut Weissert, Liz Johnston, Robert Sullivan, Jack Ross, Anne Kennedy, Ana Soto, Claire Kelly, and Matt Bowes. I am grateful to Das Hanse-Wissenschaftskolleg, Fondation Jan Michalski, *Poetry New Zealand, Alberta Views, Polyglot, Montréal Serai*, and Canada Council for the Arts.

In 2017, to honour NeWest Press' 40th anniversary, we inaugurated a new poetry series to go alongside our Nunatak First Fiction, Prairie Play, and Writer as Critic series: Crow Said Poetry. Crow Said is named in honour of Robert Kroetsch's foundational 1977 novel *What The Crow Said*. The series aims to shed light on places and people outside of the literary mainstream. It is our intention that the poets featured in this series will continue Robert Kroetsch's literary tradition of innovation, interrogation, and generosity of spirit.

CROW SAID POETRY TITLES AVAILABLE FROM NEWEST

Tar Swan — David Martin

That Light Feeling Under Your Feet — Kayla Geitzler

Paper Caskets — Emilia Danielewska

let us not think of them as barbarians — Peter Midgley

Lullabies in the Real World — Meredith Quartermain

The Response of Weeds: A Misplacement of Black Poetry on the Prairies — Bertrand Bickersteth

Coconut — Nisha Patel

How to Hold a Pebble — Jaspreet Singh

Jaspreet Singh's short pieces have appeared in *Granta, Brick, Walrus, Zoetrope, Neue Zürcher Zeitung,* and the *New York Times.* He is the author of the novels *Helium, Chef,* and *Face*; the story collection *Seventeen Tomatoes*; the poetry collections *November* and *How to Hold a Pebble*; and the memoir *My Mother, My Translator.* He is a recipient of several awards and has been translated into many languages. He lives in Calgary, the traditional territory and home to the diverse Indigenous peoples such as: Niitsitapi, Siksika, Kainai, Piikuni, Tsuut'ina, Métis, Îyâxe Nakoda. You can find him online at jaspreetsinghauthor.com